THE WHITEBIRD STORY

STORY

A CONSPIRACY OF SILENCE

By
Tom Walker

There is nothing hidden that will not be revealed nor anything concealed that will never be known.

Luke 8.17

FIRST EDITION

ISBN 978-1-68489-113-9

If you would like more copies, please contact:
Tom Walker
coloneltom1@gmail.com

Printed in the United States of America

Design and Printing: Alta-Graphics.com

Table of Contents

Acknowledgements

Of what race and breed of men are you, **Nungesser** and **Coli,** for daring to pit yourselves against a mighty ocean?

An ocean so cold and cruel that even birds may fear to fly over it.

How brave and daring of you to think you could fly across the Atlantic Ocean in a small plane made of wood and canvas, using only one engine, one propeller, and no wheels.

Now you are gone forever, your brave souls dismissing life with a smile, in the knowledge that at the time of your death you had achieved your goal and made it to the shores of the United States of America.

How shameful it is that you received no credit or reward for the brave flight that you made, and how sad it is to know that you are no longer with us in this world, lost and alone, buried somewhere in an unmarked grave.

Have no fear, for we will keep looking and searching for you until we find you.

The magnificent flight you made has kept us spellbound and led us to believe that we will all be able to fly like birds in the sky one day.

Your names will be written in letters of glory across the skies of the world.

Captain Nungesser and **Commander Coli**, we salute you.

Forward

I never wanted to be a writer or an author; sitting on my butt all day at a desk while writing a book just wasn't my cup of tea. I wanted to get out there away from the crowds and live a life of adventure instead of reading about it in books, and that's exactly what I did during the biggest part of my life.

One of my earliest adventures was in Turkey, a beautiful country but extremely dangerous if you happened to be a foreigner like I was. Working as a safari holiday tour guide, I somehow managed to get myself arrested for supposedly insulting the Turkish government, a ridiculous charge considering the fact I couldn't speak a word of Turkish.

You can read all about it and how I escaped from that country in my first book, "Run Toward the Blazing Sun."

Later in life, after sailing across the Atlantic in a 40 ft trimaran sailboat and settling down in America, I decided to become a writer simply because my grandchildren kept asking, "What did you do when you were a young man, grandpa?" But I never gave up or lost the urge to travel and experience more adventure whenever the opportunity arrived. Retirement for me was a nasty word, and just didn't appeal to me. Instead, I was continually looking for more adventure, and another story to write about that would be both interesting for my readers, and allow me to travel in this beautiful country of America I now call home.

CHAPTER 1
Arrival of Curt telling the story

The answer came when an old friend of mine, Curt, came to visit me in 2017 from Maine. "I loved your book, Tom," he said, "Run Toward the Blazing Sun. You really did have to run toward the sun to get out of that mess, didn't you? Boy, what an adventure! You were lucky to get out of Turkey alive. Well, Tom, although most people in America have guns, I think you will find it a lot safer over here, my friend.

Talking about adventure, Tom, why don't you come up to Maine next summer, visit with me, and while you are there, you could find the truth about what happened to the Whitebird and make a great book out of it? Whitebird, I said, what are you talking about, Curt? Are you serious? I don't know anything about birds.

I am a writer, not a bird watcher.

"NO NO!" Curt explained. "Whitebird is not a bird. It's a plane. Have you never heard the story of Charles Lindbergh, who was the first American to fly across the Atlantic from New York to Paris in 1927?"

"Well, he wasn't the first; the French had already beaten us to it."

Two weeks before he made that fantastic flight in his little plane, the Spirit of St. Louis, two French pilots were flying across the Atlantic coming from the other way in a plane called the Whitebird, but they disappeared off the face of the earth, and nobody ever found out what happened to them.

"I remember that story Curt," I said, but didn't they crash somewhere in the ocean?

No, Curt replied, for over fifty years, they thought they had, but there was no proof. The vast Atlantic was searched by the ships of many nations for months after the incident, but they never found anything. No bodies or wreckage was ever recovered. The two pilots, Charles Nungesser and Francois Coli, had simply vanished into thin air, like midnight ghosts.

"Well, where did they go then? Curt I asked, "I don't know for sure", Curt said. I can only guess, but I think my guess is pretty close to the truth. The prevailing winds at that time were coming from the west. So, Nungesser and Coli would have been hitting them right on the nose, that would have made it very difficult to fly and would have slowed them down quite a bit, and God helps them if they encountered any storms along the way, which I am sure they did because storms were common in the Atlantic at that time of the year.

It would have eaten up their fuel supply very quickly, just trying to stay up in the air while they were battling their way across the Atlantic, and because there was no sign of wreckage in the ocean, I think they may have actually made it to America, ran out of fuel over Washington

County, Maine, and crashed into the woods there.

"So, what makes you think they crashed in Maine, Curt?

I said.

Well Maine was, and still is, a very sparsely populated state compared to the rest of America and it's close to the Canadian border with lots of lakes and trees.

It's a documented fact that, on May 9th, 1927, the day after Nungesser and Coli had taken off from Paris, a plane was heard in the fog over Washington County, Maine by several people who had never heard a plane before in their lives.

One person in particular who heard it was Anson Berry, a local trapper and fisherman who was living in the woods by himself at the time.

His story was first mentioned in the 1980 edition of the Yankee Magazine by an author named Gunnar Hansen who said that on the afternoon of May 9th 1927, Anson Berry was fishing in his canoe on Round Lake, when he heard what sounded like an engine approaching from the North East. He couldn't see the plane because of the heavy overcast, but the engine sounded erratic and moments later, it stopped and Berry heard what he described later as a faint ripping crash.

He said that he never bothered to go looking for it because the weather was so bad, but I think the real reason was he was a loner and didn't like people.

"Anson had never seen or heard a plane before in his life, so he may have thought that if anyone was stupid enough to go up there in one of those new-fangled flying machines on a foggy day like today, they must either be sick in the head or crazy and I'm not going to get myself involved in a mess like that," why should I? I'm just an ordinary guy trying to make a living fishing and that flying up in the sky nonsense is for the birds, not for me.

"But the truth is", Curt continued, "If Anson had gone looking for it, and, we are not sure that he didn't, one of the worlds biggest airplane mysteries might have been solved".

But as it stands today, nothing has ever been reported or found of the Whitebird and its pilots since they left Paris on the morning of the 8th of May 1927.

Most people believe they disappeared in the North Atlantic, forced down by the weight of ice on their wings but on the 9th of May, over 16 people in Newfoundland saw or heard an airplane pass overhead, and another 12 in Washington County, Maine heard it also.

Given the times and locations of those accounts quite possibly, what Anson Berry had heard was the Whitebird.

Anyway, after the Anson Berry story was released in the Yankee Magazine, some people began to think that maybe the Whitebird did make it to America after all and began looking around Maine to see if they could find it.

First to arrive in 1984 was Ric Gillespie, who came to the little town of Machias and set up his Tighar organization that specializes in finding lost planes, and he began to look into the theory that Whitebird may have crashed in the Round Lake Hills area where Anson Berry first heard the plane. Using Anson Berry's story as a guide, everything seemed to be pointing in that direction.

They spent several years in the 1980s and 90s carrying out searches for the Whitebird using the most up-to-date equipment available at the time.

But in the end, they found nothing that could be connected to the Whitebird, Ric finally decided there was nothing in Maine except stories and transferred his attention to Newfoundland as the possible site of the crash.

After Ric came the famous author Clive Custler with his Numa organization who specialized in finding shipwrecks, Clive seemed to think that the Whitebird may have crashed into one of the big lakes in Maine. He managed to survey a few of them with his experienced divers, but he found nothing and so in the end he gave up and left too.

So, you see Tom, The Whitebird is still out there somewhere, Curt said. They just haven't found her yet. Many people, including me and my friend Tony have traveled to Machias several times to try and solve the mystery.

Tom, I really believe that Anson Berry's plane was the Whitebird, simply because in 1927 flying was in its infancy and no other planes were flying around the skies of Maine at that time. Anyway, there doesn't seem to be any other logical explanation for all those people hearing a plane up in the sky over Newfoundland and Maine on that particular day,

Curt said, so it had to be Nungesser and Coli. You know that old saying don't you Tom? "There's no smoke without fire.".

I think Nungesser, Coli and the Whitebird may still be laying up there somewhere in those woods just waiting for us to go and find them.

It's going to be an adventure for sure, Tom, and I know that you like adventure, but this one's not going to be easy. Wandering and searching through those woods can be a nightmare. You have to cut your way through most of it with a machete and there are all kinds of dangerous animals to contend with: moose, bears, and coyotes, to name just a few, and if that doesn't frighten you, the flies, ticks, and mosquitoes certainly will they are terrible in those woods just waiting to bite you and suck your blood.

But on the positive side Tom, if we carry guns, wear protective clothing and find the Whitebird, it's going to be worth it all in the end because the French people will be eternally grateful to us for solving the mystery of what happened to their WW1 pilots.

You know Tom, even if we find the Whitebird there won't be much left of the old gal, considering the fact she has been laying in those woods all these years rotting away, her mostly wood and canvas fuselage will have gone long ago. However, the engine, propeller, and cockpit controls should still be there.

So, are you game to come up to Maine and help me find her Tom?

WOW! what a story, I said, "you bet I am Curt, who could resist an offer like that? Sure, I'll come, but do you realize if we find the Whitebird, it's going to be one of the biggest aviation mystery stories ever told about a lost plane? Bigger than the Amelia Earhart story and it will probably change history forever by proving that Nungesser and Coli were first to fly across the Atlantic before Charles Lindbergh.

You can count on me, Curt, I said. This just happens to be the type of adventure and story that I've been waiting to get involved in for a long time, and from what you're telling me, it sounds like it's a very interesting one too.

BOY! I thought Nungesser and Coli must have been really brave to do what they did and should be recognized and honored for making such a flight. They certainly don't deserve to be laying somewhere in an unmarked grave.

"Curt, I said." Let's go find the Whitebird, and give the remains back to the French people as a gift from America. They gave us the Statue of Liberty, didn't they? Well let's return the favor and give them back what's left of the Whitebird. Let them build a statue or monument in honor of Nungesser and Coli, and maybe if their remains can be recovered, return them back home to Paris where they belong.

"Ok Tom, that sounds like a good idea, Curt said. Here is my address, I hope to see you next year in Maine," and with a wave of his hand, Curt was gone, speeding away in his little car as fast as he could go.

CHAPTER 2
Preparation and reason for the search

After Curt left, my head was in a whirl, and I began to think about what I had let myself in for. I had given my word that I would go to Maine and help but I wasn't a young man anymore, I was 78 years old for God's sake, and Curt wanted me to dance through the woods like a young teenager.

Of course, I could drive up to Maine, help Curt find the Whitebird, and write the story. It would make a great summer vacation for me and a good book, but what would be the point other than writing another book? It all happened such a long time ago, there has to be a better reason to do it than that.

But wait a minute I thought, don't I owe the French people a debt of gratitude for helping me escape from Turkey? Yes of course I do, it was those two French girls Ann and Simone, that had helped me escape from the Turks many years ago and without their help, I surely would have been killed or imprisoned in Turkey. I never got the chance to thank them for their help and solving the Whitebird mystery would be the perfect way for me to pay them back. So, I'm going to do it.

During the rest of 2017, all my spare time was spent researching the lives of Nungesser and Coli, so I could get to know them better before setting out on a new adventure to search for them, and the more I read, the more I began to realize what great guys they must have been, both fearless and brave.

Just think about it for a moment. You would have had to be fearless and brave to try and do what they did.

Imagine yourself saying goodbye to your loved ones, then climbing aboard a small plane made of wood and canvas, sitting in a freezing, open cockpit for hours on end with only one engine, one propeller and no wheels, flying across a vast ocean against the prevailing winds that nobody had ever flown across before, and finally landing in New York harbor in front of the Statue of Liberty to the adoration of thousands of people who were calmly waiting there for you to arrive. The mind boggles just thinking about such an adventure, but somehow, I don't think I would want to do it.

CHAPTER 3

Nungesser and Coli

C harles Eugene Jules Marie Nungesser was born in Paris on 15th March 1892. Brought up in a single-family home by his mother who adored him. Charles grew very quickly and at first became interested in competitive sports like boxing, and later, as a handsome young man, his interest turned to women, fast cars, and airplanes, which he quickly learned to fly by borrowing a friend's Bleriot plane.

When WW1 broke out in 1914, it was a natural choice for Charles to use his newfound flying skills to fight and defend his country so he signed up for the military, was quickly transferred into the French air force and became one of their top Ace pilots Francois Coli was born in Marseille on June 5th, 1881, to an old Corsican family with strong maritime traditions. He was an excellent student and decided to go to sea rather than pursue an academic career. In 1905 at the age of 24, he obtained a diploma at sea as "Captain of Long Distance" During WW1, he too wanted to help his country but couldn't find a sea captain's job so he enlisted in the French air force and quickly learned how to fly, becoming one of their best pilots.

Following the war, Francois became a long-distance pilot using his flying and navigating skills. On January 26th 1919 he achieved the first double crossing of the Mediterranean Sea in a plane with Henri Roget, an over-water, long-distance record.

When the Great War was finally over, everyone began moving into the 1920's, the Roaring 20s as it was called then, or by some people, the jazz age. It was a time of economic prosperity and carefree living for many people worldwide, but for Nungesser and Coli, it was not so prosperous and carefree.

People were busy rebuilding their lives after the Great War, having a good time and everybody soon began to forget about their war heroes. For instance, who would be interested in employing someone whose only job skill was flying up into the sky, shooting down other planes, and killing people?

Although Charles was an excellent motor mechanic and could have found a job anywhere doing just that, he craved more flying and adventure.

Francois, on the other hand, was ok. He was married with children and had become a first-class pilot and navigator, continuing to do what he liked doing the most, flying and navigating,

Like many other young people, Charles decided his fortune lay in America. So, he got on a ship and went there. Still young, handsome and in his prime despite his many war wounds, Charles quickly adapted to the American way of life, becoming a film actor in Hollywood. He made a movie called "The Sky raiders", where in a leading role, he got the chance to meet many beautiful women and was able to get back into a plane once again as a stuntman for the film, the part of his life that he loved the most.

CHAPTER 4
Building and flying the Whitebird

By the mid-1920s, things began to change fast. New technology had allowed airplanes and engines to become bigger in size and more powerful, able to carry heavier weights and travel longer distances, so it was inevitable that sooner or later someone would want to fly across the Atlantic to the new world by air instead of traveling the old-fashioned way on a ship. People had grown tired of traveling by sea because it took days and sometimes weeks to get to a destination.

Then there was seasickness to contend with, and what was even worse, ships sometimes didn't make it across the Atlantic at all; they sank to the bottom of the ocean like the Titanic in 1912.

To start the ball rolling, on the 1st of June 1925,

a New York hotel owner Raymond Orteig, who loved hearing stories from the young pilots arriving home from the war in Europe, renewed his cash prize offer of $25000 for the first aviator or aviators who could successfully fly nonstop across the Atlantic from New York, to Paris, or Paris to New York.

This caused quite a stir among the aviators and a lot of excitement on both sides of the Atlantic. When Charles heard about it, he thought that, with his flying skills, he could be the man for the job, and win the prize, so he packed his bags and headed back home to Paris in preparation to take on the challenge.

Teaming up with his old wartime friend Francois Coli, Charles approached the famous airplane manufacturer Pierre Levasseur in Paris and after a lot of wrangling and persuasion, they convinced Levasseur to back them in their quest to win the Orteig prize by building them an aircraft capable of flying across the Atlantic Ocean non-stop.

A new design was chosen to seat Nungesser and Coli side by side in the cockpit instead of one behind the other. The bottom of the plane was strengthened and made into the shape of a boat, so they could land on water and a new lever fitted allowing them to drop the wheels after take-off, to save weight and allow more carrying capacity for the extra fuel that would be needed on the flight.

Nungesser and Coli wouldn't be needing the wheels, of course, once they were airborne, because the plan was to land in the harbor in front of the Statue of Liberty as a tribute to France's friendship with the United States.

French newspapers started following and reporting the story, because being WW1 ace fighter pilots and heroes of France there was a lot of public interest in what they were doing and it soon became apparent that this was going to be a race between America and France to bring home the prize and honor for the winning country. During construction of the new plane, Nungesser and Coli decided to have it painted white and call it The Whitebird, in case they crashed into the sea.

The last remaining detail was to hand paint Nungesser's wartime insignia on the side of the plane, a black heart, white skull and crossbones, and a coffin with 2 candles: It was Charles' good luck charm that had helped him scare away German pilots during the war, and it worked very well because, with it, he was able to shoot down 45 enemy aircraft over the battlefields of France. Unfortunately, as you will learn later in this book, Charles's good luck charm did not help save his life when the White bird finally came down in America. It had the reverse effect.

Nungesser's insignia and good luck charm that he put on all the aircraft that he flew

Whitebird was built and completed by the 16th of April 1927 and after vigorous testing of the engine and controls by flying the Whitebird around the skies of France during the last few days of April, Nungesser and Coli were ready to proceed with the greatest challenge of their lives, an adventure that would end in their violent death.

All that was needed now was a good weather forecast and on the 8th of May they got it. With a huge crowd numbering thousands gathering there to wish them good luck, they took off at 5.17 a.m. From the grassy field of Le Bourget Airport in Paris on Sunday morning 8th May 1927. Once airborne, they dropped the wheels and headed west. With an escort of four planes accompanying them, they made their way to the French coast at Etretat and headed out into the morning mist of the English Channel. Whitebird was last seen crossing the coast of Ireland on her way west into oblivion and was never seen or heard from again. Nungesser and Coli just disappeared into the mist like midnight ghosts.

Thirteen days later on the 21st of May 1927, Charles Lindbergh completed his historic flight from New York to Paris in the Spirit of St. Louis, and became the first man in the world to fly nonstop across the Atlantic Ocean to the continent of Europe. Returning home by ship later with the Orteig prize money stuffed in his pocket and a glorious homecoming from the American people.

While unknown to the world, Nungesser and Coli were lying in a makeshift grave in Washington County Maine.

CHAPTER 5
2018 start of the search

My search for the Whitebird started in the summer of 2018 when I decided to drive from Florida to Maine in my motor home and meet up with Curt as promised so we could start looking for the Whitebird, but to my dismay, When I got there, I found that Curt had lost interest in searching for the Whitebird. "Oh! Tom," he said, "I'm fed up with that project now I've gone on to other things. I think someone may have already found and taken the Whitebird engine out of the woods, and everything else will be gone too, so I don't think it's even worthwhile looking for that plane now."

"Well thanks a lot, Curt, I said. For getting me excited about the search, and making me come here for nothing, but I'm telling you right now, I'm not giving up. Nungesser and Coli are still out there somewhere and have not been found, so I'm going to keep looking. The story is too interesting to let go. If Nungesser and Coli crashed here, Curt, I said, the French people have a right to know about it, and if they decide to exhume the bodies and take them home for a decent burial, their families should be allowed to do so.

Well, Curt said, I'm not interested anymore, it's been too long ago and nobody really cares about it. Still, being as you are so adamant about finding that plane, I will introduce you to a good friend of mine who is just as crazy as you about finding the Whitebird. His name is Tony and he is a great guy. But please promise me one thing, Tom, don't mention my full name in your book because I've got other things going on right now and I don't want to be connected with the Whitebird anymore.

Ok Curt, I said, have it your way if that's what you want, I will respect your wishes, so now, please call your friend and let me meet him as soon as possible so we can get started on the hunt for the Whitebird.

CHAPTER 6
Tony

Curt was right. Tony turned out to be a very nice, quiet, kind of guy, a retired mechanic who knew everything there was to know about engines. Tony had dealt with them all his life. He owned and lived in a nice house on the top of a hill in another part of Maine with plenty of space for all his toys. He and his older brother lived there in the house and got on very well together, but Tony was like me. He gets bored very easily and craves a new adventure now and again. He just couldn't wait to find and get his hands on that beautiful, antique, 12-cylinder Whitebird engine he had heard so much about that was supposedly lying in the woods somewhere.

"Where do you think, we should start looking, Tony?" I asked. I'm new around here in Maine, so I don't know which way to go.

Well, I think we should start looking in the Washington County area near the town of Machias, he said, there was an old hermit living in the woods about 12 miles north of there, and the records say that he was fishing on the Round Lake at the time when he heard the plane go over and crash behind the 3 round hills there."

"Curt and I have actually been there a couple of times," he said. And the last time we took along a psychic lady called Jean, who was an expert at finding murder victims for the police, Jean told us while we were camping there in the woods that it was the very spot where the Whitebird plane had come down and that we should start using our metal detectors the next day. She also said that she had seen a vision of Francois Coli in the sky above saying, "please take me home." How did you know it was Coli? We asked.

Well, Jean said, he had a patch on one eye, didn't he?

The very next day, we started metal detecting around the area, but never found a damn thing.

Maybe we should go and take another look though Tom. Tony said, because it's the only lead we have right now, and I really believe in the power of those psychics, don't you? No, I don't, I said, but I will keep an open mind about it if you think so. Let's give it a try. We won't have to camp in a tent where a bear or coyote could get us, I've got the motor home with a spare bunk in it where you can sleep, and as long as we can get the motor home near the place where we need to search, and don't get lost in those woods, we'll be ok.

No", said Tony, "I can't go right now, but you can, Tom, and I will meet you there in a couple of days. Machias is just a small town, it doesn't even have a traffic signal in the town, it's got the main street and that's about it, so I should be able to find you easily enough in that motor home of yours, then we can start looking for the Whitebird together in earnest.

CHAPTER 7
Machias and its people

O k, Tony, I will see you later then, and off I drove again into the unknown. Driving up the East coast of Maine I enjoyed the beautiful countryside and sea views before eventually arriving in the small coastal town of Machias, which was originally named by the Passamaquoddy Indians who still live in the area.

They named the town Machias, which in the Indian language means "Bad little falls' 'because on the outskirts of town, there are a couple of dangerous waterfalls on the Machias river where it empties out into the bay that could hurt you pretty bad if you tried to go down them in a canoe.

Tony was right, there wasn't even one traffic light in the town, no parking meters or anything like that. But there was one place 1 found interesting down by the bay that was famously, called the Dyke.

The Dyke was a place by the side of the road where people could come every day, weather permitting, and sell their unwanted household items, furniture, antiques, and farm produce etc to name just a few, like a flea market. But The nicest thing about it was you were allowed to set up free of charge without having to get a license or permission from the town hall.

Actually, in Machias, like many other small towns in Maine, the people are very friendly, hard-working and in most cases will treat you with respect if you talk to them nicely, but that doesn't mean to say they will accept or trust you because, unless you were born in Maine, you would never be one of them.

They are a very proud people, and even if you are an American citizen coming from another state, in their eyes, you will be classed as being from away, and considered to be what they call a flatlander, and as long as you understand that, everything will be alright.

I guess this suspicion of outsiders goes back in history to a time when the English and French settlers fought each other continuously for control of the territory that is now known as Washington County, Maine. The French finally gave up and moved across the river into Canada.

It's a funny situation really, the French and the British never seemed to like each other, and I've been told that in some areas, the attitude still remains to this day.

Having said that, I was a stranger and a foreigner myself in Machias, unarmed and close to the Canadian border, not knowing a single soul or what to do next, so I figured I had better keep my mouth shut and maintain a low profile until Tony arrives.

That first night in Machias, I slept in a local food store parking lot with the motor home and had no trouble at all. The next morning, I visited the library to check out some of the old stories and local newspaper reports that might be connected to the Whitebird. There were quite a few of them, but nothing specifically said that any wreckage had been found in the area or that the Whitebird mystery had ever been solved in Maine.

Tony showed up the next day at my motor home door with a grin on his face and a metal detector in his hand. "Let's go, let's do it", he said excitedly, "let's go and find the Whitebird".

Where to then, Tony? I asked. "Well," let's go back to the place where me and Curt camped with Jean the psychic Lady," Tony said; she was certain that it was the place where the plane had come down and afterwards saw Coli's face above in the clouds.

"OH! Tony" I said, "I don't believe in any of that psychic stuff, it's all hogwash and baloney to me, but considering we haven't got any other leads at the moment, I will keep an open mind about it and give it a try. If you think that we can find the Whitebird by using a psychic, let's go for it".

So off we went and spent several days checking out that whole area with our metal detectors, wandering through the woods, turning over rocks and digging into the swampy ground but never found anything. "Well, that was our first blank search. Tony said, "I guess Jean really has lost her psychic abilities and must have been mistaken, so where do we go from here?"

CHAPTER 8
Harvey and the Jim Reed engine

Well, I said, I was talking to a local lady at the library before you came Tony, and she told me there was a guy by the name of Harvey Hall, who lives in East Machias that has a lot of information on the Whitebird. At one time, he was working with the Tighar organization looking for the Whitebird in the 1980's or 90's. Let's go and talk to him and see what he has to say. Maybe he can give us a lead about where we can look next.

Harvey turned out to be a very friendly, hard-working guy and was pleased to see us because he was still very interested in the Whitebird story and believed that it had crashed locally somewhere. He hoped that someone would find it soon, even if it wasn't him. After talking to Harvey and pouring over his photos and research papers, Tony and I thought it would be a good idea to allow Harvey to join us as a third member of our team is searching for the Whitebird.

One of Harvey's old newspaper clippings told the story of a lady called Evelyn Magoone, who was 10 years old at the time in 1927. She was home from school and heard a commotion going on outside. When she went into the garden, she saw her brother and father pointing up into the sky at a big white plane circling her father's 90-acre farm. It was skimming the treetops like it was looking for some place to land, she said." It made a big impression on us at the time because we had never seen a plane in our lives before she said", My father, brother and me thought it was going to crash, when it suddenly took off and disappeared over the trees in the direction of love lake.

I'm going to find that lady and talk to her right away, I said. "You can't," Harvey said she's dead just like all the other witnesses, it was over 90 years ago, Tom, but she does have a granddaughter who works in a beauty shop in Callais. Maybe you could get some information from her". "Ok, I'll go and talk to her," I said.

While I was at the beauty shop talking to Evelyn Magoon's granddaughter, a lady called Beverly Reed, who was having her hair done, stood up and said, "my husband Jim Reed was the one who found the engine to that plane you are looking for,"

"What!" I said, are you serious? Yes, she said, "he was on that television program called Unsolved Mysteries a few years back talking about that engine" "Is Jim still alive?" I asked? "Yes, she said I'll give you his phone number, if you like and you can talk to him. This was the first big break we have had in our search so far.

Jim Reed turned out to be a very pleasant old man who was eager to tell us his story, and we made arrangements to meet him in a coffee shop the very next day. "I tried to tell all the other searchers my story over the years", he said, "but they wouldn't listen to me and preferred to go looking for the Whitebird in other places. I guess they thought they knew better than me, so I just let them get on with it", he said, "but I will tell you guys because I like you."

"It was 1970, and I was a lot younger then he said. I was hunting in the woods by myself and I stopped to rest in a field of rocks. Sitting and hiding behind a large rock, I was waiting for a deer to come out of the trees so I could get a good shot at him when I noticed a strange, looking rock along the tree line. Later, when I went over to check it out, it turned out to be a large aircraft engine stuck in the bank and covered with moss and gravel."

"How did you know it was an aircraft engine", we asked?

Well, I used to be a mechanic in the US Air Force, he said, and I worked for Pan American Airlines too. I know what an aircraft engine looks like and there was something else there that was very peculiar, some kind of wire, a very strange looking wire, it was half round on one side. I had never seen wire like that before.

I tried to pull it out but it was stuck under the engine and I couldn't budge it, so in the end, I just threw it down on the ground and left.

"I didn't know the Whitebird story at the time," Jim said, and I couldn't have cared less about a rusty old aircraft engine with wire around it in the woods. People dump things out there in those woods all the time, he said.

I was a young man and more interested in shooting a deer so I could carry it home for my wife.

"Could you show us on the map where you saw that engine Jim, we asked? "Sure," said Jim. It's in the Maine public reserve lands, west of Rocky Lake. In Township 18. "Perfect," we said.

By this time, we had gained a fourth and last member of our group. I will call him Jack to protect his identity. I met Jack, of all places, at a pawn shop in Calais, where I had gone to buy another metal detector for the hunt. Jack was a pleasant guy. He worked for a local Land conservation group, so Jack had plenty of experience metal detecting and knowledge of walking in the woods. He was younger than us and happily married to a beautiful Passamaquoddy Indian girl. Jack was also a gun, bow and arrow enthusiast, and wanted to join our group, so we thought why not, we could use his knowledge and experience and he could protect us in the woods. His skills would be invaluable in helping us find the Whitebird, we thought, so we let him into our group. The rest of the summer months of 2018 were spent with all 4 of us searching the area that Jim Reed had pointed out on the map.

We found the field of rocks and the tree line he had talked about, but we couldn't find his engine and wire. So, in the end, we dismissed it all as yet another false lead.

Jim Reed was genuine enough and I don't think that he would deliberately mislead us. He might have seen an engine, but we were sure it wasn't the Whitebird engine that we were looking for and it wasn't in the area where he said it was.

CHAPTER 9
Using a Psychic

It was during this time that Tony was still trying to find the Whitebird by using psychics; he saw a couple of them paying out of his own pocket, but nothing conclusive ever came from it.

We asked him each time he went, don't tell the psychic about the Whitebird or our search for it because she might make things up and lie to you, sending us on another wild goose chase looking for the plane. Just listen to what she has to say and see what she come's up with.

One psychic in particular that Tony went to see on August 7th, 2018, deserves a mention. She was a world-renowned psychic and had no prior knowledge of the Whitebird story. Here is a transcript of Tony's talk with her that he sent me:

Tony; I'm looking for two men who I believe died in the Maine woods a long time ago. So, this is a cold case file, then, the psychic said? "Yes," Tony replied. By the way, the psychic asked, "do you fly a plane?" No, Tony said, "Well then, who is that pilot standing over there? Is he a friend of yours?" After talking to the invisible pilot for a few minutes, the psychic turned around and asked Tony, where have you been sent on a fool's errand looking for that plane? And when Tony showed her the map where we had been searching, she said, "No wonder you haven't found it, you've been looking in the wrong place, it's not there, it's over here," she said, pointing to another spot on the map. "How do you know that," Tony asked? "Well, that's easy," the psychic said, "the pilot is standing right next to me telling me where it is." That was kind of creepy and when Tony told us about it, we went straight to the new spot on the map where the psychic had pointed, but again we didn't find the Whitebird.

Searching for the Whitebird in the woods turned out to be a lot of fun and adventure with the expectation of finding something. We got to breathe fresh air and receive plenty of exercise while cutting our way through those woods. But, in certain places, it was hell on earth. Slippery swamps and large moss-covered boulders as big as houses were lurking in those woods. They had rolled down there with glaciers from the ice age, and among those rocks and boulders were caves where the bears lived. But to tell you the truth, there wasn't any danger from wild animals like Curt had tried to warn me about, I never saw a bear or a moose. One day I did manage to see a small black bear crossing the road while I was driving, but nothing else, no coyotes, no wolves howling, not a sound coming out of those woods except the rustling of the trees but worst of all, no sign of the Whitebird either, not a trace.

Rocks and boulders in the woods of Main

CHAPTER 10
Thinking things over

Driving my motor home back to Florida in October 2018 to get away from the coming Maine winter, and not having found any trace of the Whitebird, I began to ask myself, did the Whitebird really crash in Maine in 1927, or am I only fooling myself into believing that it did?

How could a plane of that size painted white just disappear off the face of the earth? Designed to land on water, it was 32 foot long with a 47 foot wingspan, crashing on land or water, it would have stuck out like a sore thumb during the early days of its crash when everyone was out there looking for it. In the first few weeks following the disappearance of the Whitebird, they sent out another famous American pilot, Floyd Bennett, to search for Nungesser and Coli. He spent nine days flying up and down the coast of Maine and Newfoundland looking for them and came back empty-handed. Nungesser and Coli were wearing specially designed, fur-lined, leather flying suits to protect them from the cold. Whitebird was designed to land on water and if she had crashed in the sea or into a lake, she would have floated, her four wings would have broken off and floated, and if both pilots were killed in the crash, the bodies would have floated, almost everything on that plane would have floated, except the engine and propeller and someone, somewhere, would have discovered the wreckage.

No, the Whitebird did not crash into the sea, and she did not crash into a lake. She crashed on land and for reasons best known to themselves, someone buried or burned the Whitebird to hide it from the world, but why?

Was it the American government who selfishly covered up the story because they wanted Charles Lindbergh and America to remain the winners of the Orteig Prize, or was it local people who, for reasons of their own, didn't want foreigners and flatlanders invading their territory?

It was a well-known fact that many local people in Washington County had illegal stills making moonshine liquor during prohibition, and they wouldn't have wanted anyone snooping around on their lands. This whole thing was now beginning to look like a conspiracy, I thought, a conspiracy of silence, but by who?

Whitebird could have crashed in Newfoundland, of course, as Ric Gillespie had suggested, because it was just as unpopulated as Maine, or Whitebird could have crashed off the French Island of Saint Pierre and Miquelon as some of the French searchers believed. But if that were the case, why haven't they found anything? And what about all these people in Maine who said that they had heard a plane overhead at a time when there were no planes in Maine? Is it possible that they could all be liars? I said to myself. No, I don't think so, but there is no smoke without fire.

Spending the winter months of 2018 in Florida gave me a chance to think things over again in my head, and I couldn't wait for the summer of 2019 to come around so I could get back to Maine and continue the search for the Whitebird.

This time, however, I was going to take my little Kia Soul car instead of the motor home, so I could save gas and road toll fees on the trip.

It wasn't as bad as you might think because being a small car, it was easier to drive, easier to park and easier to sleep in after I had fitted a comfortable bed behind the driver's seat.

Getting my group back together again in 2019 and motivating them to look for the Whitebird was difficult; they all had their own lives to live, jobs and problems to worry about, except Tony, of course, who had become my right-hand man in the search. Tony, a divorced man, was a retiree like me and had done pretty well for himself financially in his retirement, so he didn't have to worry about money.

There weren't any new clues to the whereabouts of the Whitebird so we spent the best part of the 2019 summer months going back over old ground again in the Maine public lands near the rock field where Jim Reed had said the engine was, but we never found his engine or anything that could be remotely connected to the Whitebird.

CHAPTER 11
2019 Joe's Whitebird song

During this time and for various reasons when I couldn't get my group together to look for the Whitebird, I would spend my time at the Dyke in Machias, selling a few things to help with my traveling expenses and talking to local people in the hope of getting new clues to the whereabouts of the Whitebird. One day I got into a conversation with a man named Joe Pickering Jr, who, like me, was very interested in the Whitebird story. "I'm a songwriter," Joe said, and I have been writing a song about the Whitebird, with an old friend of mine. I will let you hear it when it's finished, he said. Joe was an older guy like me, so I thought he was joking when he said he was writing a song. Old guys don't write songs, do they? I thought.

Well anyway, a couple of months later, Joe called me and said he had finished the Whitebird song and it was being sung by Roger Eydenberg on YouTube." You should listen to it, Tom,"It's a beautiful rendition of the Whitebird story that you are writing about he said"? And when I heard it, I had to agree with him, it was great.

Here is a copy of the lyrics Joe and his friend Daniel wrote, I think they are fantastic.

Before lucky Lindy flew to Paris, France, the
flight of the Whitebird had New York in a trance.
Thousands waited, but they never did see,
Whitebird swoop over the Statue of Liberty.

She made her way from Paris on a history-making
flight, then the Whitebird vanished into a fog-
filled light.

Is she in the Atlantic resting peacefully, Like the
great Titanic, another tragedy?

Where is the Whitebird? Where did she fly?
Why did she fall down that day from the sky?

Is she in Round Lake Hills near Machias, Maine,

Will we ever find that ill-fated plane?
Did she fly over Newfoundland heading west,
The courage of those men guided her great Quest?
Painted white she'd be seen if she went down,
Despite all the searching, she's never been found.

Where is the Whitebird? Where did she fly?
Why did she fall down that day from the sky?

Is she in Round Lake Hills near Machias, Maine,
Will we ever find that ill-fated plane?

Where is the Whitebird? Where did she go?
Where is the Whitebird will we ever know?

Where is the Whitebird? Where did she fly?
Why did she drop down from the sky?

You can hear the Whitebird song written by Joe and Daniel being sung by Roger Eydenberg on YouTube if you click on it. It's a haunting melody, and it takes you right into the story I am writing.

CHAPTER 12
Searching banks of the streams

One day in 2019 we got another break from a local man who approached Harvey and said "I heard that you are interested in finding the Whitebird plane, I know where it is he said and its not in the woods where you have been looking," its near a stream in the wilderness and you can only get to it by canoe."What stream? Harvey said in disbelief, there are lots of streams around here.

"Go in that direction," the man said, pointing his finger, and figure it out for yourself. There is a mound, and it's less than 100 ft from the stream. I can't tell you any more, I am taking a big chance just talking to you," he said. There are others involved who don't want the Whitebird found and they will be mad at me if they find out I have talked to you.

"Please go and find the Whitebird where I have told you it is and leave my name out of it.

When Harvey told us what the man had said, we thought, maybe this was another fake story, a trick to wear us down and lead us in the wrong direction away from the truth? We had heard so many of them before but, what if this one was true?

We will just have to go and find out for ourselves and so for the rest of the summer in 2019, we got into our canoes with metal detectors and checked out all the streams in the wilderness where we thought the Whitebird may have come down but again, we came up empty handed.

This search for the Whitebird is becoming a nightmare, we thought. Where the hell is she? We know she's here somewhere, but where, and what happened to Nungesser and Coli?

Did the Whitebird really crash in Maine? So far, we have not found one single piece of evidence to prove that she even made it to America, let alone crash here.

Maybe they are all stories, maybe the people around here just like telling stories and are happy, making us look like fools searching for it.

But I just couldn't get that saying out of my head, the words kept ringing in my ears.

There's no smoke without fire. There's no smoke without fire. By the end of 2019, when I was due to go back to Florida again, the first departure from our group had begun; it was Harvey. He said he had enough but wouldn't tell us why. All he would say was, "I must not be the one to find the Whitebird." Harvey was another person who believed in psychics, so did he have a dream or a warning from a psychic telling him not to look for the Whitebird, or did someone threaten him because we were getting too close?

The funny thing was Harvey didn't mind us looking and even insisted that we continue searching for the Whitebird without him." It's here, he said, take my word for it, I know it's here, I can tell you that much, but I can't tell you the real story of what happened to Nungesser and Coli because It's terrible, too horrible to tell. You are going to have to find out for yourself. And some day, the whole world is going to know the truth about what happened to the Whitebird."

"Tom, Harvey said, 1 know you are going to write a book about all this, but please, when you write your book, don't use my real name in it. 1 am too well known around here, he said, and 1 am afraid of the consequences. They might come after me. There are some folks around here that don't want the Whitebird found and if they find out 1 am still looking, everything could go bad for me. 1 have to live with these people you know, and when you go back to Florida, you can get away from them, but 1 can't."

Wow! 1 thought there is something wrong here. Harvey had been looking for the Whitebird for many years, even before us, and was so enthusiastic about joining our group. Now all of a sudden, he decides to drop out and is afraid to tell us why. We must be getting too close to the Whitebird and he's been threatened, 1 thought.

CHAPTER 13
The dream of never give up

Back in Florida again during the year 2020, it was the worst year of our lives. Everyone had become fearful of the virus. Some of my friends had dropped dead after catching Covid and I was hiding away, writing books, wearing a mask, and keeping my distance from other people.

Finding the Whitebird was becoming an obsession with me. I was getting up there in years, but I could still hack my way through those thick Maine woods with a machete and keep up with the other guys without using a walking stick or a cane, and that was thanks to my dad, who had given me the best piece of advice a kid growing up could ever have had.

He said, "Listen, Tommy, remember one thing

all your life." Keep your head while all others lose theirs, stay alert, don't drink, don't smoke and don't take drugs because they will kill you for sure, "A man is a man only if he takes good care of himself, he said, and if you don't take care of yourself, nobody else will."

And by golly, he was right. How many men of my age could have gone through those woods and swamps in Maine? The only thing I really needed now at my age was a little more rest, and I would be up again looking for a new adventure.

My need for rest led me to take a nap one day, and I began dreaming of an incident that happened to me in the past, when I was a young man with a business taking tourists from London to Turkey in a Safari Land Rover. The Turkish government in London had distributed my brochures in their tourist office and helped me get some of the passengers, so everything seemed legal and safe to do the trip until I got to Turkey, where the government I was dealing with had been overthrown, and for taking tourists there, the local police in the town of Bodrum decided to arrest and accuse me of insulting the Turkish nation, a ridiculous charge considering I couldn't speak a word of Turkish.

Anyway, while awaiting trial, I managed to get my tourists to safety aboard a Greek boat to the Island of Rhodes before escaping myself into the mountains with my Land Rover and 2 beautiful French girl companions Ann and Simone. Avoiding all the roadblocks, I was desperately trying to make my way to Istanbul to get help from the British consul, when, one day I drove around a bend in the road, and there was another roadblock." Well, girls, I said, I guess it's over, they have seen me and will put me in handcuffs when we get into that roadblock, do me a favor, take my Land Rover and continue on your journey alone."

Ann and me, sitting on the Land Rover before entering the military roadblock.

"NO! NO! The girls said. "Don't give up" Tom, we are not leaving you. We will bluff our way through this roadblock together you will see, don't give up on us now.

And with those words, Ann and Simone began to unbutton their blouses to expose their beautiful breasts.

The young soldier's eyes popped out of his head when he saw the girls sitting in the Land Rover with their breasts exposed. He stuck a gun through the window and demanded to see our passports. I didn't have a passport, because the Turks had taken mine at the jail. So, I handed him the girls' passports instead and pointed at them saying "Tourist, Tourist French tourist," but the soldier wasn't interested in their passports, his eyes were firmly fixed on the girls' breasts. Then he quickly looked my way expecting another passport from me, so slapping my chest I hollered, "Chauffeur, Chauffeur, I am their driver," and with that the soldier still staring at the girls breasts, gave me a big grin, withdrew his gun from the window and waved us through the checkpoint. Laughing and buttoning up their blouses outside of town, the girls later said, "see Tom, we told you it would work, don't you ever give up on us again, we are going to make it out of this country together or not at all."

At that moment, I woke up and realized that I was only dreaming, but my memories were true and clear as a bell, it was what actually happened back then, and the advice Ann and Simone had given me has stayed with me all my life. I will never forget it, and I will never give up.

"Don't worry, girls, I mumbled under my breath. Now that I was fully awake, I won't give up. I'm going back next year to Maine and I'm going to find that Whitebird plane if it's the last thing I do."

CHAPTER 14
More clues and the story
of Anson Berry

After a long drawn-out 2020 with fears of the Covid virus I was finally able to get back on the road again in 2021 heading toward Maine without the motor home and without a place to sleep except in my car.

Because of the Covid crisis, a lot of rich New Yorkers who were afraid of the virus had rushed up to Maine and bought most of the available property to use as second homes leaving very little to rent but, as usual, I was lucky and found a nice cabin that needed some work owned by a lovely couple named Dora and Richard. They seemed to like me so they let me stay there in return for some painting jobs around the place. Thank you, guys.

At the end of the season, when it was time for me to leave, Dora and Richard were so pleased with my work, they said they would put a plaque on my cabin door, telling everyone that "Tom Walker, the author, had slept here."

Getting my team together in 2021 was even more difficult than before because Jack and his wife had contracted the Covid 19 virus and had to stay home in quarantine away from everybody.

So, with Jack out of the picture and Harvey gone from the group, Tony and I were the only ones left to search for the Whitebird. We talked about it and decided that if we didn't find the Whitebird this year, it would probably be our last and we would have to give up.

But in the back of my mind, I just couldn't give up. The spirit of Ann and Simone was pushing me on. "Don't give up, they whispered. "The Whitebird is there. It's got to be, and all you have to do is go and find it."

There was another clue that we began to follow. A blueberry farmer named Harold Vining, living in Cooper in 1927, heard a plane fly over. Harold, was 18 years old at the time and he was outside his parents' home chopping wood when he heard the plane. It made a big impression on him because it was the first plane he had ever heard in his life. "It couldn't have been Charles Lindbergh," he said because it was heading in the wrong direction toward Anson Berry's place, then I heard the engine cut out, it was that quick he said so it couldn't have gone far." Harold's story and commentary is on the Unsolved Mystery TV program, season 1, episode 23.

Between Harold Vining's farmhouse and Anson Berry's camp is an unmade, gravel road known as Route 19 that leads to the small township of Wesley.

A young couple named Everet and Abigail Scott were traveling along that road when they heard the plane too, so they stopped the car and listened as it flew over.

Putting these accounts together, I realized that if the Scotts had heard the plane and Harold Vining had heard the engine cut out, it couldn't have gone far. Flying as low as they were with a 900 lb engine and the weight of two pilots, Whitebird would have gone down like a ton of bricks and crashed close by before actually reaching Anson Berry's fishing location on Round Lake.

So, was it a mistake when Anson Berry told researchers that a plane flew over and crashed behind the Round Hills or did he deliberately lie about it to mislead them?

I did some research on Anson Berry. In his younger days, he was a good-looking man who came from a large local family and was happily married to a girl named Iva. In 1906 when Iva was only 21, she gave birth to a daughter but unfortunately died during childbirth.

Anson Berry, the last man to hear the Whitebird before it crashed

Anson was heartbroken, devastated, and bitter when he lost his wife, so he renounced his religion and became an atheist, saying he couldn't believe in a loving God that would allow his young wife to die in childbirth.

Anson gave the child to his sister to bring up, then in 1909, he traveled out west to Montana to be a logger and a cowboy until 1916 when he returned home briefly to give his daughter $5 to buy some candy which in those days, was a lot of money. He then went back to Montana and his brother Carl followed him, but the next year 1917, Anson returned home alone, and no one ever found out what happened to Carl.

Anson immediately went into the woods to live by himself as if he was hiding from someone or something. Building a log cabin on the riverbank near the Wigwam ripples, he became a tough, hardened trapper and fisherman, keeping mostly to himself and becoming feared by many of the people in the area.

It was said that if anyone tried to build a cabin in his territory, even if they were members of his own family, he would burn them out, just like they used to do in the old days. Everyone became afraid of him.

Traveling into town occasionally by canoe, Anson would pay for supplies that he bought from a local store with pieces of gold. Nobody knew where he got the gold from, and most people were too scared to ask, but it was a known fact that the Whitebird was carrying some gold when she left Paris.

It was on such a trip into town in 1936, 9 years after the Whitebird had crashed, that they found Anson Berry dead in 2 feet of water at a dock on Hadley Lake, his canoe loaded with supplies, was floating nearby.

The official coroner's verdict said that he had a heart attack, fell out of his canoe and drowned.

But another story or rumor circulating at the time said they found him in the water with his hands tied behind his back and his head bashed in. But after so many years, who knows what the real truth about that story is?

CHAPTER 15
Breaking the conspiracy of silence

2 021 and the last year of the search. With only Tony and me left to do the searching, there were no new clues, and both of us were at our wits end trying to figure it out.

When by some divine miracle, act of God or just pure luck, I managed to stumble upon the truth of what had happened to the Whitebird, where she had crashed, and what had happened to Nungesser and Coli. All those years before in 1927.

I was in Machias that day, waiting to meet up with Tony again. It was a hot summer day, so I went into a bar by myself and ordered a cold drink. Sitting at the bar, I began talking to a couple of local guys who were curious to know what I was doing in town.

'Oh! I am just an English writer, I said, and I'm here to write a new book about a plane called the Whitebird that was supposed to have crashed around here years ago."

Both guys were very interested in the story, but when they left, and before I had a chance to finished my drink, the waitress walked over and said to me, "I heard what you were talking about with those two guys, and I want to tell you something, I know where the engine is to that plane you are looking for, it's in a sawmill. I don't know which sawmill because there are lots of them around here, but they have got it in a sawmill, for sure."

WHAT! I replied, how do you know this?

Well, she said, I was married to a man whose family held a terrible secret about that plane. After it crashed, my husband's grandfather was one of those involved in killing the pilots and stealing the gold that they were carrying. They removed the engine, and put it in a sawmill before burning and burying the rest of the plane to cover up their crime.

The area and ground where the Whitebird crashed is in the wilderness, and it's wet and soggy there, so they couldn't dig graves for the pilots. Instead, they put them back into the cockpit and covered it over with elder bushes and branches so that it couldn't be found. There's supposed to be a mound there even to this day.

Why are you telling me all this I said, staring at her with my mouth wide open?

"Well, my husband told me this story because I was his wife. She said I loved him, and I was trusted with the secret because I was now part of his family. He is a proud man, like most of them around here. He loved his family and his family's heritage, but the knowledge of what his grandfather had done disgusted him and messed up his mind.

Even as a child, they had brainwashed him to shut up and keep quiet about it, but he knew it was wrong and, as a result, grew up angry and bitter himself. He started beating and ill-treating me, I couldn't stand for that so I ended up divorcing him.

So, you see, the reason I can tell you all this, she said, is that I no longer have any love or loyalty towards my ex-husband or his family and can tell you the secret of the

Whitebird, the way it was told to me."

Do you know where the Whitebird is buried? I asked, "No she said, he never took me there, but I do know you can't get to it by road; you have to go up a river in a canoe.

Look, she said, I know this sounds crazy, but don't take my word for it, here is my ex-husband's address, go and talk to him yourself, he lives with another woman now and maybe, if you are lucky and catch him in the right mood, he will tell you the whole story I think he wants to get it off his chest.

When Tony came along, and I told him what the waitress had said, he couldn't believe his ears. "We never expected our search to end this way. What an awful thing to happen, he said. Why didn't Harvey tell us this story? He must have known the truth. That's why he said he must not be the one to find the Whitebird.

I'm going to have to interview that husband I said, and see if I can get the truth out of him if his story matches his ex-wife's, we will know for sure that the story is true, and we can finally put an end to the search for the Whitebird.

"No, Tom," Tony said," you can't go and see her ex-husband, he might be a dangerous man."

Look Tony, I said," I may be an old man, but I'm 6 ft 4 inches tall, 220 lbs, and I've been around this world for a long time so I'm not scared to go and talk to anyone, except maybe a Turk with a loaded machine gun."

"Well, let Jack do it then," Tony said, he is younger than us, he's got some authority in this town and can take care of himself. He used to be a policeman, you know. Let him do it."

"But we can't let Jack do it, " I said; he's caught the Covid virus and is in quarantine with his wife.

I'm going to have to see him by myself, Tony, I said, we can't wait any longer, someone's gotta do it, and it might as well be me, and anyway I'm bigger than you." Well, be careful, then Tony said. I'll wait for you here."

When I arrived at the ex-husband's house, I didn't know what to expect from him or how he would react to a stranger with a funny accent. He was a big guy like me, only younger .and I thought he might slam the door in my face or throw me out on my ear, but he didn't.

Actually, he was quite a friendly, hospitable guy, not at all like his ex-wife had described him to me.

I started a conversation with him, basically by telling him the truth, that I was an English writer and I had come to Maine to write a story about some of the old families that live in the area and had chosen his family to write about because I knew many people with the same name back in England who would be thrilled to hear about their cousins in America.

Once I had him feeling at ease with me and not seeing me as a threat, I sprung the question on him and asked point blank. "What do you and your family know about the plane that crashed here" years ago?"

I watched him as the blood slowly drained from his face and the tears began to well in his eyes before he suddenly blurted it out, "I loved my grandfather, I love my family, and I am a proud and loyal son, he said, but they killed those brave pilots, shot them dead and they shouldn't have done that he said,

Those pilots were heroes, they had done something no man had ever done before and our family, including myself, have had to live with it and keep quiet about it all these years, carrying the shame on our shoulders to protect my grandfather and others while the whole world has been wondering what happened to those pilots; he said, it's not fair.

I've known about it since I was a child, listening to their conversations behind closed doors, and when I was only 8 years old, I was asked at school to write an essay about something, so I wrote about the Whitebird, proudly bringing it home to show my grandfather.

When he saw it, he went crazy, tore it up in front of me and threw it on the floor, and then with a loud voice, he shouted "DON'T you ever write or talk about that Whitebird plane again." I was shocked and terrified because I didn't understand I loved my grandfather, and I had never seen him angry like that before. The incident has affected me my whole life ever since.

Tell me about the plane crash. I said, what did your grandfather tell you about it?

"Well, he said, some of my family including my grandfather, were fishing at the time. It was foggy and overcast that day when the plane came down, it was like a huge dragon falling out of the sky they said. It hit the bank on one side of the stream and then the other, breaking in half behind the cockpit.

None of my family had ever seen a plane in their lives before and when they saw that insignia on the side of the plane, a black heart, skull crossbones and a coffin, I think they got scared and shot them, stole the gold they were carrying, took the engine and put it in a sawmill before realizing that the plane had flown across the Atlantic and the whole world was looking for it. So they got scared and quickly burned and buried everything they could to cover up what they had done, and It has been kept a secret in the family ever since.

"Do you know where the Whitebird is buried, I asked, and can you show me on this Google earth map?" I said, "yes, he said it's right there pointing to a specific place on the map. You can't miss it. There is a mound."

At the end of our conversation, I began to realize that my informant must have been the same man who's conscience wanted him to tell his story to Harvey about the Whitebird back in 2019, telling him it was up a stream. We went looking for it at the time but somehow didn't get close enough.

"Well, thank you so much for telling me all this," I said, to my informant," you are a very brave man, for finally breaking the conspiracy of silence surrounding the Whitebird that has been holding you and your family in chains all these years. I'm glad you have finally got it off your chest."

"Some of your family members may be mad at you when they find out you are the one who has spoken up about this tragedy, but one day they are going to understand that what you did was the right thing to do for everyone concerned, your family and the descendants Nungesser and Coli.

"The story would have come out anyway, sooner or later, and it's just not fair that you, or any of your family, should have to keep it secret and carry the shameful burden of what your ancestors did.

Goodbye, I said to my informant, and good luck. I hope that everything will be better for you in your life now "But before I go, I want to tell you one thing, the Whitebird story will be told, I don't know if anyone is going to believe it but one way or another it has to be told so, that the world can know the truth of what happened to those 2 brave men.

'But I'm making this promise to you now that I will not publish or print your name in my book".

A couple of days later I took Tony to meet my informant and he told him the same story, so it looks like our search for the Whitebird had finally come to an end.

CONCLUSION

Dear reader, 1 have tried to write this book as truthfully and as accurately as possible, bearing in mind that there are no witnesses left alive who can verify the real story. 1 can only say that 1 followed my instinct, and wrote down everything that 1 heard and saw, changing only some of the names to protect my friends and informants. It was never my intention to name and blame anyone or any family for what their ancestors have done in the past, especially as many of them today were not even born at the time these events took place.

If you think about it long and hard it all makes sense. There were 16 people who heard or saw a plane in Newfoundland on May 9th 1927 and 12 more who heard it in Washington County Maine. Most of them in those days had never heard a plane in their lives before so it made a big impression on them at the time. Where did it go? And why hasn't it been found? After reading this book I think the answer is obvious and all it took was the breakup of a marriage and a brave man willing to tell the truth.

Made in the USA
Middletown, DE
19 June 2022